# HAYNES EXPLAINS
# THE HOME

## Owners' Workshop Manual

© Haynes Publishing • Written by **Boris Starling**

Published in October 2017

A catalogue record for this book is available from the British Library

ISBN 978 1 78521 157 7

Haynes Publishing, Sparkford, Yeovil,
Somerset BA22 7JJ, UK
Tel: +44 (0) 1963 440635
Website: www.haynes.com

Haynes North America, Inc.,
861 Lawrence Drive, Newbury Park,
California 91320, USA

Printed and bound in Malaysia

Cover image from Getty Images

Illustrations taken
from the Haynes MGA
Owners Workshop Manual

Written by **Boris Starling**
Edited by **Louise McIntyre**
Designed by **Richard Parsons**

# Safety first!

More accidents happen at home than anywhere else. Nails get hammered into digits; ladders are fallen off, especially when descending from the loft with an armful of Christmas decorations; rugs are tripped over; and hot cups of tea can scald. It's ironic that there are so many personal safety regulations applicable to cars, building sites and so on, but so few in the home. Then again, hard hat and hi-vis tabard in bed is never a good look.

# Working facilities

Working facilities can vary greatly according to the precise parameters of the home in question. A small urban studio flat may be only $10m^2$ and therefore exempt from the Cruelty To Domestic Animals Act (Section 34 Clause 2: Room To Swing A Cat). A stately home may boast a dining table 200 metres long with his Lordship and her Ladyship sitting at opposite ends and communicating via the butler (who can't wait for the day they discover Snapchat).

# Contents

# Introduction

We are as a nation obsessed with the home. You can hardly turn on the TV without Kevin, Kirstie, Nick, Phil or Sarah popping up at the head of yet another property programme.

For as any fule kno, an Englishman's home is his castle. The home is a source of great pride, great effort and great expense. Almost every part of the 'home process' has its pitfalls. Getting a mortgage can be so convoluted and frustrating that you begin to believe that Franz Kafka is not dead but alive, well and working in the customer services department of your mortgage provider. Dealing with difficult neighbours can involve the kind of persuasive skills usually deployed at the tensest and most complex stage of governmental power-sharing agreements or peace treaties. And both interior design and maintenance may look deceptively easy, but if you wonder how far wrong it's really possible to go with a paintbrush, a spanner and a hammer – well, give it a go and find out.

But all the troubles and heartache are worth it when you have your home just the way you want it – at least for those few minutes before you think 'actually, I wonder if it would look better if...'.

# About this manual

The aim of this manual is to help you get the best value from your home. It can do this in several ways. It can help you (a) decide what work must be done (b) tackle this work yourself, though you may choose to have much of it performed by external contractors such as the builders who turn up when they like or the interior designer who presents you with a dizzying array of swatches and colour schemes and has an impeccably polite way of telling you that your taste stinks.

The manual has drawings and descriptions to show the function and layout of the various components. Tasks are described in a logical order so that even a novice can do the work. Although the specific requirements of the home can vary according to age, socio-economic status and region, fundamentally they are all variations on the following: somewhere which is just a little nicer than the home of the neighbours you like and a lot nicer than that of the neighbours you loathe.

# ⚠ Dimensions, weights and capacities

## Overall height

| | |
|---|---|
| 16th-century cottage, ceiling............ | 5'9". They weren't just short back in those days. They were hobbits. |
| Georgian rectory, ceiling.................... | 11'4". Good for making the room light and airy. Bad when it comes to changing the battery in the smoke alarm. |
| Top-floor flat in Victorian building..... | 50' above ground. With no lift. And heavy shopping. |

## Overall weight

| | |
|---|---|
| Of a mid-size family house ................. | c. 50 tons. Plus 2 tons if they haven't thrown out all their old CDs yet. Plus another 2 tons if they have a 65" curved QLED TV. |

## Consumption (Energy Performance Certificate)

| | |
|---|---|
| 'A' rating (92+) ..................................... | very energy efficient. Become honorary member of the Green Party. |
| 'D' rating (55–68)................................. | averagely efficient. Mid-table. The Stoke City of EPCs. |
| 'G' rating (1–20)................................... | Woeful. Even Chinese factory owners think you're environmentally unacceptable. |

## Engine

| | |
|---|---|
| Stroke................................................... | usually caused by the stress of dealing with mortgage companies. |
| Power .................................................. | liable to be cut in rural areas during high winds when a tree falls on the power line. |
| Torque ................................................. | of property prices at dinner parties, mainly. |
| Bore...................................................... | the DIY obsessive who knows everything. |

# People carriers

Most people will have tried communal living (i.e. with people who aren't immediate family members) at some time in their lives, whether it's at university, in the early years of work before people pair off and settle down, or in a strange modern building with brightly coloured furniture and a disembodied Geordie voice which says things like 'day 44 in the Big Brother household'. Here, Haynes Explains offers ten top tips to ensure your housesharing doesn't go all Pete Tong, and also gives a handy guide to the kind of housemates you're likely to come across.

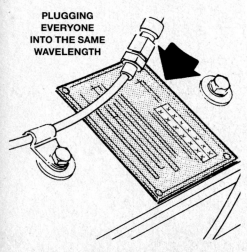

**PLUGGING EVERYONE INTO THE SAME WAVELENGTH**

FIG 11•1 **COMMUNICATION BREAKDOWN AND HOW TO AVOID IT**

**1)** It's tempting (especially being British) to let tensions fester and build up without ever mentioning them, let alone addressing them. Don't. The tensions won't go away: they'll get worse. Nip them in the bud by discussing them openly and reasonably.

**2)** That said, choose your battles. If you're always sweating the small stuff then it'll be much harder to get your way on the big stuff. And a lot of the stuff is small stuff (or at least stuff which is down to differing interpretations: one man's slob is another man's Zen master).

**3)** Clean up after yourself. Don't leave any communal area dirtier than when you found it. In the kitchen, no discarded yoghurt pots or dirty dishes. In the living room, no pizza boxes or crumpled newspapers.

**4)** Give each other space and be sensitive to each other's needs. The early-to-bed brigade won't appreciate endless Playstation bleeping at 1am. Those for whom the day does not start without ten cups of coffee won't appreciate in-depth breakfast discussions about Western liberalism.

**5)** There are always one or two housemates who do more work around the house than the others (they're the neat freaks). They probably don't mind doing this, but they do mind being taken for granted, so once in a while express your gratitude by buying them a small gift. Alcohol or chocolates is good. Cheap petrol-station flowers are just about OK. A handheld vacuum cleaner is taking the piss.

**6)** Keep a proper list of spending and split it fairly and openly. Money causes more arguments than anything else, even snoring and unpleasant boyfriends/girlfriends who stay over and then act like they own the place (Note: check that they don't actually own the place, or else you might be looking for somewhere new to live after a frank exchange of views). You may choose to designate one flatmate as official bill payer who in turn collects money from everyone else.

**7)** Assigning fridge and cupboard space can be as tricky as the task facing Empire-era civil servants tasked with dividing up far-flung provinces without causing civil war (they mostly failed). Defend your own space, because if you don't then no one else will. And label everything.

**8)** When it comes to your housemates' possessions, remember the 3 'R's: resist, request, replace. Resist use of their stuff. If you can't resist, then request – ask them whether you can borrow/swipe. And always replace, like-for-like.

**9)** Have a 'free shelf' for items which anyone can have (food about to expire, stuff you don't like, or offerings made in the spirit of peace on earth and goodwill to all men.

**10)** Use technology. A WhatsApp group and/or shared electronic calendar mean everyone knows what's going on at all times (and is also useful for banter which in turn helps keep things light). There are plenty of apps like HomeSlice, WunderList and SplitWise for helping with communal finances and stock taking.

**At its best, housesharing can be brilliant, full of deep friendships and quickfire banter. At its worst... well, it can be terrible, like a second-rate soap opera made reality.**

# Passengers

### The Spoilt Brat

Has rich parents and a job which is part-time/non-existent. Spent their gap year in India or Thailand and still goes on about it. Has more clothes than everyone else put together but still nicks everyone else's – without asking – and moans about having nothing to wear. Behaves with such a sense of entitlement that at times you wonder whether they are not so much a real person as a piece of performance art. And if you think the Spoilt Brat is bad, just wait till you meet their friends....

### The Slob

Has two main positions: prone on the sofa and prone on their bed. Never offers to help, though in fairness never seems to see or be bothered by any of the dirt either. Big on: takeaway food, computer games, boxsets, tracksuit bottoms, bare feet. Not big on: personal hygiene, exercise, motivation, work. Biggest risk: that one day The Slob will just fuse with the sofa at a molecular level, like a sci-fi/horror film, and never be able to escape. Mind you, he'd still be happy as long as he had a pizza and Netflix to hand.

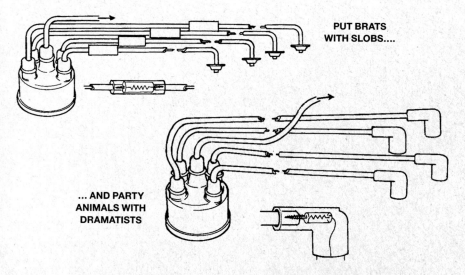

**PUT BRATS WITH SLOBS....**

**... AND PARTY ANIMALS WITH DRAMATISTS**

FIG 11•2 **CONNECTION BOARD: ENSURING THE RIGHT MIX OF OCCUPANTS**

## Mr/Ms Activity

Never just sits still and chills by slumping in front of the TV and talking good-natured crap like the rest of the house. No: Mr/Ms Activity is always doing something self-improving. When you're in the pub, they're helping out at the soup kitchen. When you're in bed with a hangover, they're on a 12-mile run. They're always bouncy and gleaming and smiling and really nice. The best thing you can do with Mr/Ms Activity is hope they find love with another Mr/Ms Activity, so they can become the Activities and go on weekend orienteering trips around the Brecon Beacons while you contemplate the world's largest fry-up.

## The Party Animal

No matter how late you go to bed, the Party Animal will still be up. And no matter how late you get up, the Party Animal will still be in bed. If the Party Animal ever asks you out for 'a quick drink', beware. Be very ware. The Party Animal has lots of friends, many of whom you will meet when you find them passed out in various locations in your house (though you're unlikely to get much sensible conversation out of them). He/she also pulls off the mysterious trick of always having enough money to go partying but never enough to pay their share of the household bills.

## The Dramatist

Everything in their life is a drama, to be recounted in excruciating detail – the horrible boss, the feckless friend, the temperamental lover. It's like all the Canterbury Tales at once. For them, life is either the end of the world or the best thing ever, and they expect you to go along with whatever is applicable at that precise moment. The tendency to overact and overreact also manifests itself in day-to-day housesharing, where they can fly off the handle at the slightest pretext (yet weirdly they can also take genuinely serious setbacks in their stride).

THE ENDLESS WHEEL
OF SELF-IMPROVEMENT

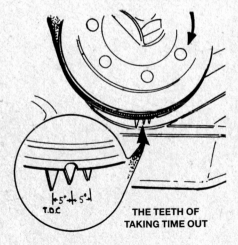

THE TEETH OF
TAKING TIME OUT

FIG 11•3 **PINNING DOWN MR/MS ACTIVITY**

# The car next door

Just as there are certain types of housemates, so too are there certain types of neighbours. Some are good neighbours, the kind that Aussie TV made a soap opera out of.

### 1. The over-friendly neighbour
Well, they don't seem so at first. At first they just seem nice and friendly. But gradually they want to know all about your life, and your family and your job and your friends, and when you're away they'll volunteer to pop in just to check on things, won't be that often, just three or four times. An hour.

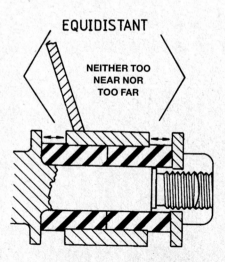

EQUIDISTANT

**NEITHER TOO NEAR NOR TOO FAR**

FIG 11•4 **THE GOLDILOCKS ALGORITHM: PERFECT NEIGHBOUR PROXIMITY**

### 2. The fighting neighbours
With each other, usually. Starts with raised voices and, depending on the time of night and the amount of drink which has been taken, ends with the kind of crockery-smashing more usually associated with Greek weddings and/or the police turning up.

### 3. The noisy lovers
(These can even be the fighting neighbours once they've made up.) They go at it hammer and tongs at all hours of the day and night, and at a decibel pitch that even commercial aircraft aren't allowed to attain. After a while you'll know their routine and be able to impress your guests by saying 'trust me, they're nearly done' and, as the screams from next door reach fever pitch, adding 'and… and… and… yes, all done.'

### 4. The mysterious neighbour
Never says very much. Keeps odd hours. Never has any friends round. If you do have to knock on their door, they'll open it the bare minimum so you can't see anything inside. They're probably harmless, but if they are ever outed as a serial killer you'll be first in front of the cameras to say you always knew they were a wrong'un.

## 5. The borrowing neighbour

As with the over-friendly neighbour, it starts off all perfectly normal – a cup of sugar, a splash of milk – and before you know it you've gone through phase 2 (tools, books, DVDs) and are now well into lending them your stereo, your car and your spouse, only one of which you'll ever get back.

## 6. The party neighbours

Like the Party Animal housemate, but 10 metres further away. If you ever try to remonstrate with them, they are liable to either invite you in (and thus make you feel a real square and party pooper for trying to stop them having fun) or threaten violence.

## 7. The nosey parkers

The kind of people who ensure that net-curtain manufacturers never go bust. Usually older (retirement gives excellent opportunities for snoopers), they keep the kind of tabs on your comings and goings of which GCHQ would be proud. In fact, they may actually be GCHQ agents. Foil them by ensuring you live as dull a life as possible.

## 8. The inconsiderate parkers

As in the ones who double park, block your drive or park their car right in front of your house even – especially – when there's a perfectly good space right in front of their own house.

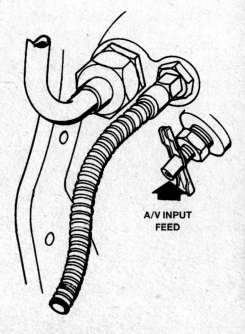

**A/V INPUT FEED**

FIG 11•5 **THE NOSEY PARKERS' DIY SURVEILLANCE APPARATUS**

### The Joneses...

...up with whom you will never quite keep. Their car will always be newer and shinier than yours, their lawn more perfectly manicured, their clothes more expensive and ostentatiously designer. It's a game which has no end and which neither side will ever acknowledge even exists.

### 9. The gossipy neighbour

May double as the nosey parker, but sometimes not (sometimes they're in league together). Knows everybody's business and is keen to share it. If they ever tell you that your secret's safe with them, try to get inside before you burst out laughing. You'd be better off taking out a personal slot on the local radio than telling them anything.

### 10. The neighbour with dogs which bark endlessly

A tie here between the ones who make no attempt to get their dogs to be quiet and the ones who do – the first because it's just irresponsible, and the second because it rarely makes a difference and in fact usually causes more noise rather than less.

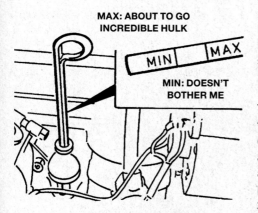

MAX: ABOUT TO GO
INCREDIBLE HULK

MIN: DOESN'T
BOTHER ME

FIG 11•6 **TOLERANCE GAUGE FOR NEIGHBOURLY CANINE/ MUSICAL NOISE**

### 11. The boundary nitpickers

God forbid that even a leaf from the tree in your garden should extend over the vertical plane marked by their fence. And God forbid that if it really bothered them that much they could just lop it off rather than come round to yours in high dudgeon to demand you do something about it right away (but obviously without giving you access to their side of the fence, which would make it a lot easier).

### 12. The musical neighbour

Actually, not even the musician, as in certain circumstances a musical neighbour can be rather agreeable. The wannabe musician. In particular, the wannabe guitarist who thinks he's Slash and the wannabe drummer who thinks he's Keith Moon. Mate, you're not and you never will be, no matter how many hours you practise and how insane your repetitive error-laden scales drive everyone else.

### 13. The fireworks fans

There's a time for fireworks, and that time is (a) Guy Fawkes Night (b) New Year's Eve. Setting them off at any other time should be a crime on a par with sedition and treason. On the plus side, the sound of 20 people from 20 different households standing in 20 different back gardens yelling 'SHUT UP!' is even more impressive than the average fireworks display.

# ⚠ Urban living

| Pros | Cons |
|---|---|
| Cheap transport. Moan about tube and bus fares all you like, but running a car is way, way more expensive. | Expensive accommodation. As in REALLY expensive, especially in London. A shoebox right above the boiler? That'll be £450 a week. |
| Cheap heating. Flats and houses tend to be small, and cities keep the heat better than the countryside. | If you drive a 4x4, you will look ludicrous. The nearest that most Chelsea tractors get to going off-road is the Waitrose car park. |
| No one knows your business. For a place with so many people, the city can offer a surprising amount of anonymity. | No one knows you. This can be lonely, especially if you've moved to a new city far from your home or uni mates. |
| Cities have great energy, which can make you feel enlivened. | The criminals also have great energy. Petty crime – and sometimes not so petty crime – is commonplace. |
| You're never more than 400 metres from a cool bar or café. | You're never more than 400 metres from a crack den. |
| There are lots and lots of good jobs in the city. | There are also lots and lots of people going for those jobs. And lots and lots of people packed in like sardines going to and from those jobs on public transport every day. |
| You can hardly move on Sunday mornings for farmers' markets. | Only billionaires can afford their prices. |
| There are nightclubs so you don't have to stop drinking at 11pm. | But you do have to stand in line for an hour while a pair of bouncers give you the sneer. |
| Shopping. Good shopping. Great shopping. | Pollution. You only get two coughs a year, but one lasts for seven months and the other for five. |
| Whatever your race, religion or sexuality, the city has something for you. | Good luck getting a doctor's appointment in the next three months. |

# 4x4 or city car

Forget north vs south, the Beatles vs the Stones or Rangers vs Celtic. The real rivalry in British life today centres on where you make your home. Town or country? Urban or rural? Both sides have pros and cons. And neither side seems especially keen to see beyond the stereotypes of the other. For most urbanites, rural dwellers are all carrot-crunching shitehawks who have the kind of family trees which don't fork, who know everything about tractors and nothing about the outside world. For most rural dwellers, urbanites are mollycoddled crybabies who couldn't survive a night in the wild, pushy

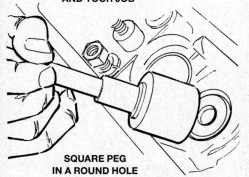

CHECK THE LIFESTYLE
SUITS YOU, YOUR FAMILY
AND YOUR JOB

SQUARE PEG
IN A ROUND HOLE

FIG 11•7 **HOW TO MAKE SURE YOU LIVE IN THE RIGHT PLACE**

## Another way

There is, of course, a solution to the age-old city/country divide. A place where every house looks the same, where Sunday morning sees a dangerous drop in the communal water pressure as everyone washes their cars at the same time. This place is, of course, suburbia: and the only thing that city and country dwellers agree on is, no matter how bad the other place is, suburbia is even worse.

hustlers always in a hurry, and litterbugs who assume someone else will pick up whatever they drop. (Rural folk will tell you with some pride that when 400,000 members of the Countryside Alliance staged a march in central London in 2002, the Metropolitan Police thanked them for leaving Hyde Park cleaner than it was when they arrived.)

**How to tell a townie in the country: they think 10am is an acceptable time for breakfast.**

# ⚠ Rural living

| Pros | Cons |
|------|------|
| Cheap accommodation. Well, certainly cheaper than the city. What buys you a tiny flat in London gets you five bedrooms and half an acre in the country. | Expensive transport. Unless you fancy waiting three days for a bus, you have to drive everywhere. Petrol, servicing, repairs – they all add up. |
| Village names. English country village names sound like minor Dickens characters or American serial killers. Dorset alone can boast Bradford Abbas, Burton Bradstock, Gussage St. Michael, Osmington Mills and Ryme Intrinseca. | Expensive heating. Country homes are often bigger, older and less well-insulated than their urban counterparts. Heating oil and logs don't come cheap. Thank heavens for the traditional British response to the cold – 'just put another sweater on.' |
| It's lovely in summer. Really, seriously lovely. The English countryside on a hot day is as good as it gets. | It can be bleak and grim in winter. And summer loveliness can pale if you live on a tourist route bumper-to-bumper with caravans being driven at 35mph. |
| Real farm shops selling real farm produce, and not at extortionate prices either. | Broadband speeds vary from tortoise to semaphore. In some areas 'reception' is something you have after a wedding rather than anything to do with communications. |
| Textbook rural pubs as your local: low timber ceilings, roaring fire, proper ale…. | … until the locals stop talking when you come in and look at you like they do in *An American Werewolf in London*. |
| There's a real sense of community, and everyone knows you. | There's a real tendency to gossip, and everyone knows your business. |
| You can get to know nature properly rather than just via David Attenborough documentaries. | Nature includes mud, and mud is everywhere in the countryside. Last day at Glastonbury is standard Tuesday afternoon for most rural dwellers. |
| You can go and see films and plays, just as you can in the city. | Well, not 'just as you can in the city'. The films are on a rickety old projector in the village hall, and the plays are put on by the local am-dram society and last five hours. |

# Upgrading

Want a bigger house without the time, expense and massive hassle of actually moving? Welcome to the home extension, keeping Polish builders employed since 2004. On the face of it, home extensions are win-win: you increase the size and value of your house in one go, and all without having to pay lawyer's fees, agent's fees, removal fees and stamp duty. Your neighbours may be less keen, particularly in certain parts of London where there are more extensions going on than in Kim Kardashian's hair.

## Getting started

Before embarking on a home extension, there are several things you need to consider. For a start, you'll probably need extra insurance, as your standard home insurance is unlikely to cover a bunch of builders coming in with RSJs and 4x2s while sucking their teeth and saying 'who did all this, then? John Wayne?' The builders themselves should have insurance, of course, but better safe than sorry. If there's one thing worse than dealing with insurance assessors when your house has collapsed, it's not being in a position to deal with them when your house has collapsed.

**YOU'LL NEED A BIT MORE THAN SUPERGLUE, MATE**

FIG 11•8 **HOW NOT TO SECURE AN EXTENSION TO THE REST OF YOUR HOUSE**

## WARNING

*During the period of the works, you must always wear a hi-vis tabard and a hard hat. This may not be a legal requirement, but most men like to pretend that it is, in order to justify the wearing of such personal protective equipment. Fashionistas: try to colour co-ordinate tabard and hat. Either orange/orange or yellow/yellow. Orange/yellow or vice versa is not a good look.*

# ⚠ Ways to extend your home

### 1. Out

An extension into the garden or a side return. If you lived in a country with a decent climate then you could probably sit in the garden for a few months a year, but since you don't you need an extension.

### 2. Up

A loft conversion. Let's face it, you're only using the loft to store all your old CDs and photo albums. (For those of you under 12, CDs and photo albums are what we used to have before iPhones.)

### 3. Down

A basement conversion. See above re storage, though in this case it's some old cement gone hard, some old paint gone hard, and a couple of old power tools which didn't work when you left them down there and aren't going to have suddenly undergone some miraculous mechanical resurrection after two years in subterranean damp.

### Remember

Builders can be cheap, quick, good or honest, but never all four at once. When considering which firm to go with, be sure to ask them for their quotation for the work (a definite price which should be itemised) rather than just an estimate (which is not legally binding and just what it says – a rough guess.) Even if you don't need planning permission, you will need to comply with building regulations. Make sure you know your legal obligations in terms of structural integrity, fire safety, energy efficiency, damp proofing, ventilation and the precise tea strength and sugar ratio for the builders' liquid refreshment.

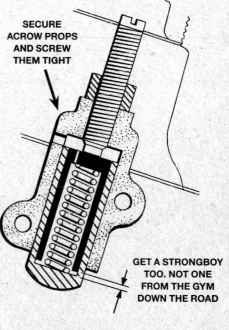

SECURE ACROW PROPS AND SCREW THEM TIGHT

GET A STRONGBOY TOO. NOT ONE FROM THE GYM DOWN THE ROAD

FIG 11•9 **ENSURING THAT ALL SUPPORTED WALLS ARE, ER, SUPPORTED**

# Constituent parts

In this section Haynes Explains looks at some of the main rooms in any home. If you have a home cinema, a basement swimming pool, an indoor bowling alley or a ballroom, then very regrettably we don't have the space to include suggestions for these (at least we don't until we get round to doing Haynes Explains Billionaires.)

### The kitchen

The kitchen should be the default centre of family life, and as such should be warm and inviting. But a kitchen also needs space for people to walk between large static points such as tables, islands, ovens and fridges. Keep knives out of children's reach and food out of dogs' reach (but not the other way round: the children will get the food anyway and dogs don't really know what to do with knives). A hanging pot rack frees up space and offers the endlessly amusing possibilities of tall people clanging their heads like cartoon characters smashed in the face with a frying pan.

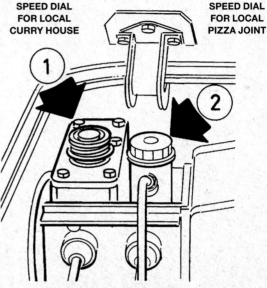

SPEED DIAL FOR LOCAL CURRY HOUSE

SPEED DIAL FOR LOCAL PIZZA JOINT

FIG 11•10 **MALE-ONLY COOKING MADE SIMPLE**

**The average kitchen contains 71 different utensils. Some are fairly niche (cheese slicer, orange presser). Some are pretty important (saucepan, knives, forks). But only one is absolutely vital: the corkscrew.**

## The bedroom

Bedrooms are used mainly for two things, and Haynes Explains knows that you're all grown-ups and don't need that explained to you. The bed is almost always the largest single object in the room, so position it in the best place to allow enough space in the rest of the room and, if possible, a good view from the bed out of the window (this last bit applies more if you overlook rolling fields than if you overlook an industrial estate). If privacy is important to you, consider how much of the room can be seen from the landing outside when the door is open. If you're a shameless exhibitionist, don't bother.

## The bathroom

Bathrooms are often small and functional. If space is at a premium, avoid encroaching on it still further – make sure shelves and cabinets are recessed, towel bars are on the back of the door, and so on. Clear shower enclosures rather than frosted glass or solid curtains give a sense of more space, as do larger floor tiles with fewer grout lines and wall tiles which run high up towards the ceiling. Make sure that the door swings out rather than in. A bathroom with a window is for obvious reasons better than one without. If you only have space for a small bath, forgo that bath and fit a large shower instead.

## The living room

This room more than others is often used for more than one purpose – watching TV, relaxing, entertaining friends and so on. Think about these various uses when arranging furniture and lighting. Living rooms are usually occupied during the afternoon and evening more than the morning, so think south-westerly rather than north-easterly aspects if possible. If you have outside space, try to directly connect the living room to this space via patio doors or similar.

**WITHIN EASY REACH
OF BEER CAN...**

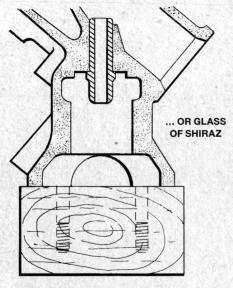

**... OR GLASS
OF SHIRAZ**

FIG 11•11 **OPTIMAL PLACING OF
THE BATH IN THE BATHROOM**

### The home office

Working from home is increasingly popular these days (as indeed is 'working from home' when you just happen to be at home on the Friday before a bank holiday weekend and/or a day where a great sporting event is taking place and you expect your boss not to notice the coincidence). If you're going to spend a lot of time here, make sure the home office is set up as well as your workplace office is. Is your chair comfortable and ergonomic? Can you close yourself off from the rest of the house? Make sure there's plenty of light. Paint the walls whichever colour makes you feel most energetic and inspired. Add personal touches to avoid making the place look soulless and corporate. Hide and/or bunch power cords as much as possible. Place the top of your computer screen at eye level or a little below, and your keyboard so that your forearms are parallel to the floor. A little fridge in the corner is good for keeping milk and soft drinks cold. But not beer or white wine. Oh no. Definitely wouldn't want those in the home office.

**If you have space, put a comfy armchair in there too, to give you a place to relax and clear your mental space for creative thought. At least, that's what you tell your spouse.**

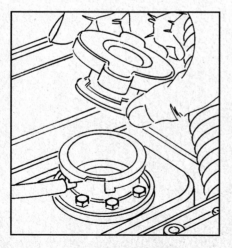

OPEN BOTTLE.
POUR LARGE GLASS.
CLOSE BOTTLE
AGAIN

FIG 11•12 **THE IMPORTANCE OF REHYDRATION WHILE WORKING FROM HOME**

# ⚠ The mancave

Sometimes in the main house, sometimes an outbuilding such as a garage or shed. A space where the male word goes. Very possibly the only space left where it does. In the mancave, the man is allowed to return to university or childhood (for many men the two are more or less the same, full of irresponsibility and vomiting) by talking rubbish with his mates, watching martial-arts films and spending hours discussing England's perennial left-back problem. Women may be banned from the mancave altogether or allowed in only on strict observance of the Mancave Rules.

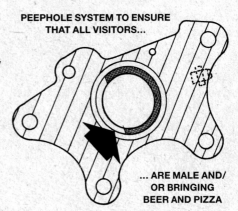

**PEEPHOLE SYSTEM TO ENSURE THAT ALL VISITORS...**

**... ARE MALE AND/ OR BRINGING BEER AND PIZZA**

FIG 11·13 **SECURITY AND ENTRANCE PROCEDURES TO THE MANCAVE**

**a)** All décor and decorations are chosen by the man.

**b)** Standards of cleanliness are set by the man.

**c)** You can never have too many Star Wars figurines.

**d)** TV screens must be at least as big as the Angel of the North.

**e)** No movie starring Jennifer Aniston may be shown.

**f)** There are only two food groups in the Mancave: pizza and beer.

**g)** Breaking wind is a competitive sport.

**h)** Scratch and sniff is permitted, but only on oneself.

**i)** The toilet seat must always be left up.

**j)** All anecdotes must be exaggerated.

**k)** All jokes must have been told at least a dozen times before.

**l)** All disputes must be settled by arm wrestling.

# Vehicle interior

Getting your interior to look the best it can is critical. Chaps, this section is especially for you, since for most of you the concept of 'interior decoration' involves chucking a couple of cushions on a sofa and saying 'yeah, that looks better.' There are lifers in jail who make more effort with their surroundings than you do. (Then again, when a woman asks her husband which one of two or more decorative options he prefers, the correct answer is always the one she most likes. Either he agrees with her or he's wrong.)

Here are Haynes Explains' top interior-decoration tips. They won't help any man get his way, but used judiciously they may help him convince his wife that he has actually thought about the issue a little rather than just shrugged and said 'yeah, whatevs.'

**a)** Lighter colours make a room feel larger. Darker colours make a room feel smaller.

...................................................................

**b)** Mirrors are always good to add light and give the impression of space. But beware using too many mirrors in a small room. No one wants to be sitting on the toilet and see multiple reflections of themselves stretching away to infinity. Horror film franchises have been founded on less.

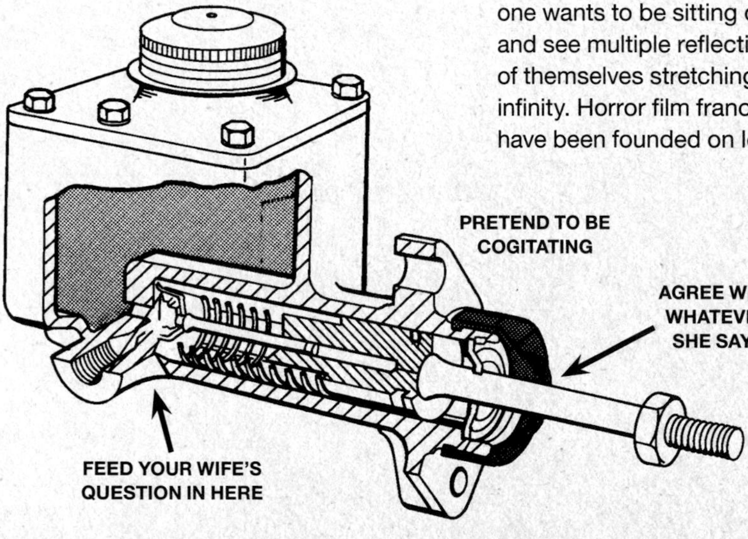

PRETEND TO BE
COGITATING

AGREE WITH
WHATEVER
SHE SAYS

FEED YOUR WIFE'S
QUESTION IN HERE

FIG 11•14 **COLOUR CO-ORDINATING MACHINE FOR MEN**

**c)** Mix it up. Patterns, textures, old, new, expensive, cheap. If you want corporate blandness, go and stay in a chain hotel. (Note: you must mix with care. Simply chucking a whole bunch of stuff together is not 'mixing'. It's 'chucking'.)

**d)** Go natural. Put flowers and plants in various rooms – they look good and add colour. Don't overdo it, though. You don't want guests thinking that they're in a garden centre or the Vietnam Jungle.

**e)** Don't overcrowd a room. Too much furniture is just as bad as too little. But in general remember that furniture breaks up a room and makes it more interesting.

**f)** Bookcases take up wall space and are more versatile than you think when it comes to decoration. You can mix books up with ornaments and photos, sort them by the colour of their spines (especially good for the OCD sufferer) and even lay some bigger books flat to break up the visuals.

**g)** Details make design. Those little touches on chairs, tables, sofas, wall hangings, even light switches and nailheads really make a difference.

**h)** If you have wooden floors, use rugs to add warmth and colour. You may wish to anchor the rugs under chair or table legs at their edges, or else risk a pratfall/banana-skin moment when you come in bearing a tray of drinks and find the rug skids away from under your feet.

**i)** Lighting is crucial – not just the way a room is lit but the shape and size of the lights themselves. Well-chosen lampshades and standard lamps can add greatly to a room. Make sure the lighting isn't too bright and harsh – it's not an operating theatre (and if it is then you're definitely reading the wrong book) – but also not too Stygian.

**j)** Be quirky. Have fun. Be creative. Something personal which makes you smile is always worth having in a room.

**Don't push all your furniture up against the wall unless you're having a party. Let it float in the room. Not literally, of course. Not unless you live in an area prone to floods.**

# Paintwork

This is one of those things which everyone thinks they can do. Lick of paint here, lick of paint there, Bob's your uncle. Except it's not that easy. Actually, it is that easy, but it won't necessarily look good. Unless you know what you're doing, you'll make your average painter-decorator look like Michelangelo ('right, mate, no messing around but you've been painting this ceiling for four years now and the Pope's getting the right hump. How much longer you gonna be?')

Preparation is key here. Before you even think about painting a wall, you need to make sure that wall's ready for the paint. Fill in any cracks, scrape away any old paint, check for mould and loose grouting and all that business. When you do start painting, make sure you have enough undercoats and coats, and remember that good-quality brushes, rollers and paints are well worth the expense. Paint cheap and paint twice.

The most sensible course of action is – yes, you've guessed it – to call a painter.

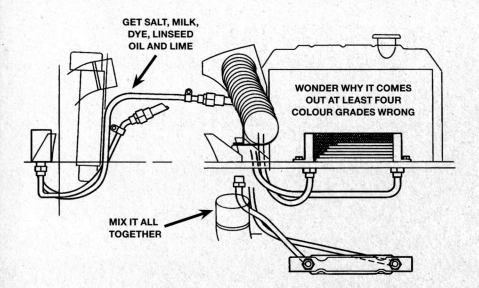

GET SALT, MILK, DYE, LINSEED OIL AND LIME

WONDER WHY IT COMES OUT AT LEAST FOUR COLOUR GRADES WRONG

MIX IT ALL TOGETHER

FIG 11•15 MIX AND MATCH – HOW TO MAKE YOUR OWN PAINT COLOUR

# ⚠ The colour charts

Actual car manufacturers like to give their paint colours names which reek of dynamism and energy: Lava Orange, Thunder Grey, Panther Black. Domestic paint manufacturers, on the other hand, adopt a more free-and-easy attitude to naming their products. Farrow & Ball, for example, have Smoked Trout, Elephant's Breath, Clunch and many similar others in their range. To this end, Haynes Explains offers the following 50 paint colour names free of charge to anyone out there who's just a bit bored of Blossom, Primrose and Lilac. Some have pretty obvious hues attached to them: others you can just freestyle.

1) Ambassadorial Chocolate
2) Angry Toddler
3) Benny/Bjorn
4) Boardroom Breakdown
5) Brexit
6) Budget Airline
7) Cilla Black
8) Clammy Handshake
9) Corbyn's Beard
10) Cowpat
11) Curdling
12) Dorkwood
13) Economy Mince
14) Embarrassing Uncle
15) Emporio
16) Final Demand
17) Five O'Clock Shadow
18) Gladiator
19) Gordon Brown
20) Jason Orange
21) Kitty Litter
22) Magaluf
23) Miami Vice
24) Micra Mauve
25) Midlife Crisis
26) Mobility Scooter
27) Nairobi Dusk
28) Nappy Needs Changing
29) Navel
30) Papercut
31) Placenta
32) Pub Ceiling
33) Rabbi Lionel Blue
34) Rees-Mogg
35) Riviera
36) Roadkill
37) Scab
38) School Cabbage
39) Scunge
40) Slurry
41) Smoker's Teeth
42) Snowbonk
43) Stargate
44) Tan Line
45) Tear-Stained Diary
46) Teenage Contempt
47) Trump's Hair
48) Urban Massage
49) Urine Sample
50) Varicose Vein

# Tackling repairs

As the great poet Robert Browning said: 'a man's reach should exceed his grasp, or what's a heaven for?' When it comes to DIY, however, when a man's reach exceeds his grasp – well, that's what A & E's for.

A penchant for DIY is deep within man's DNA. It probably harks back to Neanderthal times, when Mr Caveman would come home from a hard day's hunting and hang a mammoth's horns on the stone wall of his cave for Mrs Caveman and all the little Cavemen to admire. Little did he know that in millennia to come his descendants would spend happy Saturdays discussing the relative merits of tough American Black & Decker versus German bad boy Bosch.

There can be no DIY without the power tool. And not just any old power tool. No: the professional DIYer requires an entire set of power tools. Combi drill, impact drill, professional jigsaw, circular saw, angle grinder.... to certain people, this is not a list. This is poetry. This is love. An angle grinder might not remember your birthday or whisper sweet nothings into your ear, but then again nor will it shout at you for being home late or get jealous when you look at other angle grinders.

So what exactly can a man do with this tool? (Settle down at the back there.)

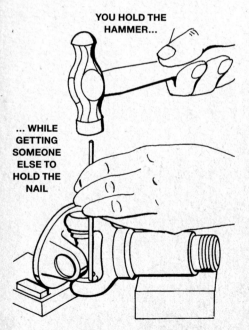

YOU HOLD THE HAMMER...

... WHILE GETTING SOMEONE ELSE TO HOLD THE NAIL

FIG 11•16 **STOP! HAMMER TIME! DIY WITHOUT SELF-INJURY**

**If you wish a man to return home quickly, send him a text saying either that you've turned up the thermostat or put his power tools on eBay.**

## Plumbing

Before you start any plumbing DIY, make sure you know where your shutoffs are. Your insurance company is less likely to pay out for flood damage if you give as the reason for said damage 'owner decided to be a have-a-go plumbing hero'. You should know not just where the various minor shutoffs are but also the main one too – the Master Shutoff, the One Shutoff To Rule Them All. You should also know exactly how long it takes you to sprint there.

When it comes to plumbing, prevention rather than cure is always best. Make sure that all appliance connections are tight and not leaking. Regularly check washing-machine hoses. Look for signs of water under sinks, around fixtures and near appliances. Check ceilings and walls for any evidence of roof leaks. Remember that most blockages can be cleared by nothing more than a plunger, and remember too that

**a)** sink plungers and toilet plungers are different
**b)** you should have both
**c)** you don't want to confuse the two. You really don't want to confuse the two.

If there's anything more serious than this, the most sensible course of action is to call a plumber.

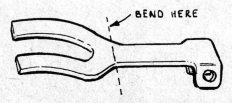

FIG 11•17 **MAKESHIFT PLUNGER. EMERGENCY USE ONLY**

## Electrics

Electrical work you should feel confident undertaking yourself:

**a)** changing a light bulb
**b)** changing a plug
**c)** turning a light switch on and off
**d)** turning a dimmer up and down
**e)** turning your Sky box on and off

Electrical work you should outsource to a professional:

**a)** everything else.

# WARNING

*Unless you really know what you're doing, don't mess around with electrics. If you do, then sooner or later you'll end up being hurled across the room with your hair standing on end like Don King or Yahoo Serious. The most sensible course of action is to call an electrician.*

# Going green

The Queen is reputed to have told a guest at a Buckingham Palace garden party that 'it's so nice to have a garden in central London.' It's a fairly safe bet that, even if you don't live in central London, your garden will be smaller than hers and you will have fewer staff to help tend it. But no matter how big or small it is, there are plenty of things you can do to keep your garden shipshape (if that isn't too hideous a mixing of metaphors).

**MAKE SURE PATHS ARE NON-SLIP. IT RAINS SOMETIMES IN BRITAIN, YOU KNOW**

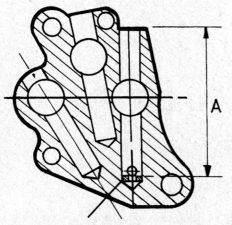

**LEAVE PLENTY OF ROOM BETWEEN FLOWERBEDS**

FIG 11•18 **DESIGNING THE PERFECT GARDEN: A SCHEMATIC**

**a)** Overwatering plants is as bad for them as underwatering. It's not the plant itself but the soil around it which will let you know if the plant needs watering. If the soil's moist, leave it be.

**b)** Plan your garden. Same difference as with 'mixing' and 'chucking' in interiors. A little bit of forethought will make a garden look ten times better.

**c)** Use the internet judiciously. At its best, it can be an invaluable source of advice and tips. At its worst, it will give you an inferiority complex from looking at too many pictures of beautiful professional gardens. Like glossy magazine food shots or porn stars' breasts, such photos are often no stranger to artificial enhancement.

**d)** If you want basic plant bargains, supermarkets are as good a place as any. If you want knowledgeable answers to your questions, go to a nursery. (A plant nursery, that is, not a child nursery, where you certainly won't get knowledgeable answers unless your question involves the wheels on the bus.)

**e)** An empty patch of soil won't stay that way for long. If you don't put a plant there, nature will put a weed there.

.....................................................

**f)** Protect newly planted specimens from slugs by putting down used coffee grounds. Slugs hate caffeine as it makes them produce too much slime which then dries them out. That's why you never see a slug drinking Red Bull.

.....................................................

**g)** Don't underestimate the therapeutic benefits of seeing things grow. The inexorable and repetitive slowness of nature is the perfect antidote to our increasingly hectic lives. And you won't get it all right first time, or even tenth time. Gardens are always works in progress.

.....................................................

**h)** When mowing the lawn, cut a wide collar (border around the perimeter), so when you start mowing across or up and down, you can turn the mower round at each end without bashing into a fence or flower bed.

.....................................................

**i)** Cutting the lawn too short is called 'scalping', and like the original it's neither pretty nor healthy.

.....................................................

**j)** Alternate the direction of cut from week to week.

## *Barbecues*

During the 72 hours of sunshine to which the British fondly refer as 'summer', there will be barbecues. Whereas 96% of men happily cede all normal cooking duties to their wives, 100% of men demand full and unquestioned control over all barbecue action. I Am Man, See Me Grill.

The fact that even in such circumstances the woman buys the food, makes the salad, prepares all the necessary tongs, plates, cutlery, sauces, bread, napkins, drinks and so on beforehand (and does all the washing-up afterwards) is irrelevant. The man has:

**a)** put the meat on the grill
**b)** burned the meat so thoroughly that it can be identified only through sophisticated carbon dating
**c)** removed the meat from the grill.

Nothing else matters. For this triple triumph, he expects the kind of standing ovation usually reserved for Oscar winners.

**I Am Man, See Me Grill.**

# Financing your vehicle

For most people, accommodation is the single biggest expenditure in their day-to-day lives, sometimes accounting for more than 40% of their total income. Here, Haynes Explains looks at some of the main ways you can approach your own property situation.

## Buying

+ you own your own place
+ you can do what you like with it in terms of decoration etc.
+ your property should (hopefully) appreciate in value over time
- you have to pay stamp duty
- if you have a mortgage, you're probably at the mercy of interest-rate fluctuations

## Renting

+ you're not responsible for maintenance and repairs
+ you have the freedom to up and leave when the tenancy's over
+ rent can often be cheaper than mortgage payments
- a bad landlord can make your life a misery
- you may be forced to move through no fault of your own

## Squatting

+ cheap. Very cheap. Very very cheap
+ Often in good neighbourhoods which will annoy the neighbours
+ Interesting housemates
- police and/or private security may 'ask' you to leave at any time

FIND THE RIGHT AREA. LOTS OF STUDENTS = GOOD. DESERTED STEELTOWN = BAD

FIND IDEAL TENANTS. PROFESSIONAL COUPLE WITH NO KIDS = GOOD. BIKER GANGS = BAD.

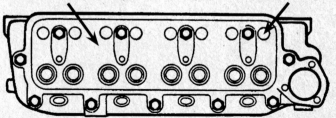

CONCENTRATE ON RENTAL YIELDS AND KEEPING PROPERTIES OCCUPIED. EVENTUALLY RETIRE TO MARBELLA WITH YACHT

FIG 11•19 **THE GREAT BUY-TO-LET LANDLORD CALCULATING MACHINE**

# ⚠ Applying for a mortgage

**A** *Get your deposit in order.*

*Arrive on exchange day. Two minutes before exchange, vendor raises the price by £20,000. You wish all manner of hateful stuff on vendor. Vendor is unrepentant. Sale falls through. Find a new place.*

*Find the place of your dreams. Put in an offer on the place of your dreams. Have offer accepted on the place of your dreams.*

*Through prayer, persuasion and perseverance, get mortgage sorted.*

*Get all necessary paperwork in order (bank statements, payslips, proof of address, electoral roll).*

*Have survey done. Survey reveals problems. Renegotiate value yet again.*

FIG 11•20

*Try and choose between fixed- and tracker-rate mortgage. Read as much as possible on stock markets and Bank of England interest rates. Become totally bewildered.*

*Try to get valuer and/or vendor to change their minds. Succeed, eventually.*

*Mortgage provider sends someone round to value the property. Valuation is wildly at odds with the offer you made.*

**B** *Have mortgage offer approved in principle. Rejoice. Briefly.*

# Selling the vehicle

Quick disclaimer: there are some good, decent, honest estate agents out there. But as with a taxi when it's raining, good luck finding one. In the popular imagination, estate agents rank somewhere between politicians and serial killers. They're seen as unscrupulous, devious, deceitful, insincere, hypocritical and venal, and those are just their good points. They wear shiny suits, splash on way too much aftershave and drive ridiculous branded superminis which any right-minded person wants to throw bricks at. They'd kill their own grannies for a sale and have more

tricks than Paul Daniels: forcing buyers into using their own in-house mortgage brokers, overvaluing properties to entice buyers to sign up, encouraging gazumping, inventing rival buyers to push offers up, showing you properties you don't want, and so on. Everyone hates estate agents. Even estate agents hate estate agents.

Most of all, they can't speak English. They speak Agentish, which might sound like English but isn't. Allow Haynes Explains to translate some common phrases from Agentish into English for you.

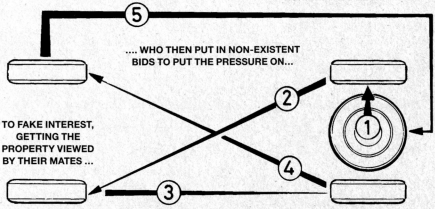

FIG 11•21 **SCAM OF THE EARTH – ESTATE AGENTS' TRICKS**

# ⚠ Speaking agentish

| Agentish | English |
| --- | --- |
| Purpose-built residential development. | Sink estate. |
| Cosy. | Tiny. |
| Easy to maintain. | Tiny. |
| Bijou. | Tiny. |
| Rural location. | 45 minutes from the nearest village. |
| Excellent transport links. | 50 feet from the M5. |
| Newly priced. | Reduced. |
| Reduced. | Desperate. |
| Offered with no onward chain. | The owner's just died. |
| Garden flat. | Basement. |
| Potential for modernisation. | Last updated during the Crimean War. |
| Tremendous scope for improvement. | Derelict. |
| Ideal as a buy-to-let investment. | In a terrible neighbourhood. |
| Within easy reach of local schools. | Gang fights on your doorstep at 3.45pm |
| Character features. | Low ceilings. |
| Three-bedroomed property. | Two bedrooms and a cupboard. |
| Viewing recommended. | It looks terrible in every photo ever taken. |
| Studio. | Prison cell. But less spacious. |
| Colourful history. | Haunted. |
| Lively neighbourhood. | The police are always round. |
| Friendly neighbourhood. | Curtain-twitchers. |
| Low maintenance garden. | Concrete slabs. |
| Exposed beams. | The ceiling has collapsed. |
| Benefits from (e.g. 'walls'.) | Has. |
| Boasts (e.g. 'walls.') | Has. |
| Split-level mezzanine sleeping. | Bunk bed. |
| Ideal for first-time buyers. | Cheap. |

# ⚠ Fault diagnosis

| Fault | Diagnosis | Treatment |
|---|---|---|
| Wrong paint colour | The man has chosen it | Let the woman choose it. |
| Floor flooded | Bath is overflowing | Turn off bath tap. |
| Estate agent talking rubbish | He's an estate agent | No treatment available. |
| Property not as described | It's the estate agent's fault | See above. |
| Mortgage provider wants more info | Mortgage provider ALWAYS wants more info | Give them everything you have. Including your old photo albums. |
| Landlord being unreasonable | Why else would he be a landlord? | Find incriminating photos of landlord in order to persuade him to play ball. |
| Power tools not working | Your wife has removed the batteries for your safety | Bow to her superior wisdom. |
| Entry to mancave barred | You are not a man | Bring beer and pizza. |
| Builders are two months late | They are builders | No treatment available. |
| Builders charge twice as much as they said they would | They are builders | No treatment available. |
| No shop within 5 miles | You have moved to the country | Move back to the city. |
| No green space within 5 miles | You have moved to the city | Move back to the country. |
| Neighbours making too much noise | They are newly-weds and at it like rabbits | Wait a few months. It'll soon wear off. |
| Neighbour making too little noise | Who knows? | Just enjoy it. |
| Clearly marked food in communal fridge has gone missing | You live with a thief | Inject your next batch of food with listeria. But remember before eating it yourself. |
| Home office not conducive to working | It's a warm afternoon. You've been working hard | See that comfy chair in the corner? It's saying 'forty winks'... |

# Conclusion

Home is very important to most people. Being settled or unsettled where you live can filter through to every other aspect of your life. If you live somewhere you love – not just your flat or house, but the neighbourhood itself – then you always have a sanctuary to return to no matter how bad your day at work or elsewhere is. If, on the other hand, you don't like where you live, then you will always be trying to find excuses not to be there rather than to be there.

Getting your home how you want it is unlikely to be an easy process. If you rent, you may probably never fully have things your way. If you own, you will be forever wondering how come keeping a house maintained is so expensive. And if you need to move to find your dream home, you will soon see why moving house is ranked only slightly below death and divorce on the list of life's stressors.

Ironically, for something so central to your well-being, your home is never finished. Just as people change and lives evolve, so too do homes. You think you have it all sorted, and then you see a magazine feature or an item in the flea market or something at a friend's house and you think, hang on…. And that's even before you factor in the influence of other people who come into your life, be they a partner who moves in and/or the patter of tiny feet (children, that is, unless you're Snow White, in which case they're probably a bunch of dwarves hoping very much that she lives on the ground floor).

Our language is full of idioms which reinforce the importance of home. Home is where the heart is. Carrying your spouse across the threshold. Make yourself at home. Home and dry. Home run. Home sweet home. No place like home. East, west, home's best. Home truths. Home fires burning. Lights are on but nobody's home. (Well, maybe not that last one.) Wherever you are, we hope your home is just that – not merely a flat or a house, but a home full of love and laughter.

## Titles in the Haynes Explains series

Now that Haynes has explained The Home, you can progress to our full size manuals on car maintenance (to get you to and from said home), *Victorian House Manual* (vintage approach), *Kitchen Upgrade Manual* (time-for-an-update approach) and *Home Plumbing Manual* (hopefully-not-too-wet approach).

There are Haynes manuals on just about everything – but let us know if we've missed one.

**Haynes.com**